A maD medley of Milligan

Other titles by the same author:

Fiction

CLASSIC ADVENTURES ACCORDING TO SPIKE MILLIGAN

THE MURPHY

BLACK BEAUTY ACCORDING TO SPIKE MILLIGAN

FRANKENSTEIN ACCORDING TO SPIKE MILLIGAN

THE HOUND OF THE BASKERVILLES ACCORDING TO SPIKE MILLIGAN

TREASURE ISLAND ACCORDING TO SPIKE MILLIGAN

Children's fiction and poetry

A CHILDREN'S TREASURY OF MILLIGAN – CLASSIC STORIES AND POEMS

BADJELLY THE WITCH – A FAIRY STORY

Non-fiction

THE FAMILY ALBUM – AN ILLUSTRATED AUTOBIOGRAPHY

Other related titles

SPIKE MILLIGAN – A CELEBRATION

THE GOONS – THE STORY

A maD medley of Milligan

Spike Milligan

This edition first published in 2003 by
Virgin Books Ltd
Thames Wharf Studios
Rainville Road
London
W6 9HA

Reprinted 2003, 2004

First Virgin hardback edition published in Great
Britain in 1999 by Virgin Publishing Ltd

ISBN 0 7535 0779 X

Typeset by TW Typesetting, Plymouth, Devon

Printed and bound in Great Britain by
Mackays of Chatham PLC

CONTENTS

GUNGA DIN

Gunga Din
Was very thin
Hardly skin and bone
He was the water carrier
To the famous seventh Queen's
     Own
'Tho' we've flogged you
And we flayed you
By the living God that made you
You're a better man than I am
     Gunga Din'
Gunga Din
Was far from dim

Sued the seventh Queen's Own
To the tune if you please
Of ten thousand rupees
So now, they leave him alone
'Tho' I've flogged you
And flayed you
By the living God that made you
You've a richer man than I am
    Gunga Din.'

HOW

My father was an Elephant
My mother was a Cow
How I got here
I don't know how

½ mile
CUT FLOWERS
½ CUT FLORIST

VAN GOGH

With hand signals
And a polite cough
He bid twelve million
For a Vincent Van Gogh
For that sort of money
I'd cut my right ear off

THERE **IS** ENOUGH ROOM TO SWING ONE. — Spike Milligan.

SOMETHING

I saw a piece of something
What it was I cannot say
You see that piece of something
Was going the other way
Suddenly that piece of something
Turned round and back again
I just couldn't see it
Because of the rain
Just then that piece of something
Shot up in the air
As far as I know that something
Is possibly still up there

ELEPHANT

I tried to paint an Elephant
But he kept moving away
I don't mind painting an Elephant
If only he would stay
That silly Elephant
Spilt it over the floor
So the only thing that I could do
Was go and buy some more
But I'm sad to say
They'd run out of Elephant Grey.
The Salesman said I've something
    else I think
I've lots and lots of Elephant Pink

So I painted another Elephant
  pink all day
But when the Elephant painted
  grey
Saw the Elephant of pink
They said My God we've had too
  much to drink.

ROBIN HOOD

Robin Hood was not
A very good shot
Despite what history said
At the Archery Fayre
The target was there
But he shot himself instead

Millionaire Prankster.

Adolf Hitler
Dictator And Clown

PART ONE

Germany

In 1909, Hitler fell on bad times. 'Fuck zis,' he said. He ended up on the streets, hungry, homeless, surviving on hand-outs of soup and living in a shelter for the destitute. He had the arse out of his trousers. 'Nein. I haff ze arse out of borrowed trousers. Fuck zis.' True, he had pawned his own trousers with arse out of them, for one mark. He used this as a down payment on a sausage, of which he ate a piece day after day. He noted in his diary, March 3rd, 'Halfway through sausage, feeling gut.' He sang, 'If I ruled ze world hefery day would be ein bright sunny day . . .'

1913, he moved to Munich, the arse still out of his trousers. 'Fuck zis,' he said. He told friends he intended to enter the Munich Art Academy. 'Hi ham going to henter zer Munich Hart Hacademy,' he said. He did enter but was told to 'Piss off.' But he fell in love with the city: 'Vimen can vait,' he said.

He had neglected to register for military service, and was arrested. He was found medically unfit for the Army. He opted for the Navy. The recruiting Boson asked him, 'Can you swim?' Hitler said, 'Vy, haven't you got any ships?' Hitler volunteered for the Army. He became a regimental runner; it was dangerous work.

'Fuck zis,' he said.

He was blown up. 'Hif I knew vot was good for me I would haff stayed hup.' He was awarded the Iron Cross. He insured himself against fire, floods or subsidence. In a gas attack he was blinded, and walked over a cliff. 'Fuck zis,' he said.

After zer var he joined the Workers' Party, which was coming apart. Using superglue he put it together, warning them to, 'Bevare of the Chews [Jews]. They trink babies' blud!' This was outrageous. Jews drank Kosher wine and tea.

October 1919. Hitler made his first speech. It went something like this: 'Bevare of the Chews, zey drink babies' blud.'

His performances, such as the vast staged spectacles of the Nuremberg rallies, were overwhelming. He never lost sight of his objectives in a speech: 'Bevare of the Chews.'

Before a speech he asked questions to which his audience could only answer yes or no, like, 'Har you alife or dead?' He was bolstered by propaganda in newspapers, pamphlets, Institutes for the Blind, Salvation Army, RSPCA, police and railway stations.

Hitler used aeroplanes to enhance his image, parachuting, descending like a Messiah. This image was spoilt when he landed in a tree. 'Fuck zis,' he said.

Earnet Rohm led the Nazi Brown Shirts, Pink Trousers and ballet shoes. Hitler's company was unsavoury misfits, hunchbacks, sexual bandits, ex-convicts, decadent aristocrats, bus drivers and policemen on point duty.

By 1930 Hitler spoke to huge rallies, the Boy Scouts, Wolf Cubs, Girl Guides and Brownies. There was a particularly sexual relationship twixt him and his audience. 'Lies! All lies. I didn't gif ein fuck about mein audiences.'

The Nazis planned a march on Berlin. Hitler was uneasy about this. He was persuaded it would work with support from the Army. The march was a fiasco, Hitler distinguishing himself by his lack of heroism. The Bavarian Police opened fire killing sixteen. 'Fuck zis,' said Hitler. He was imprisoned for five years; he served only nine months. During this time he wrote *Mein Kampf* with 164,000 grammatical and syntactical mistakes. On his release he was feted. His company (Adolf Hitler and Co. Ltd) was sought by the rich and famous. He spent weekends with Winifred Wagner, granddaughter of his idol. Hitler was a vegetarian and was given a plate with a date, three prunes, two mushrooms and cuttings of grass. 'Your breakfast, Adolf,' said Winifred. 'Vonderbar, mein leibling,' said Hitler, tucking into the feast. Hitler enjoyed support among wealthy Germans, but Nazi funds remained a mystery. Hilter kept his Post Office savings a secret. 'Anytime I feel, I can always put mein hand on five marks, nein?'

In the 1930s Hitler enjoyed Mercedes limousines, apartments in Munich, two-prune lunches and popularity with women. Of the seven women thought to have had affairs with him, six committed suicide. 'You zee? I leaf zem alone for a few months and zey commit suicide!' One was Renate Mueller, a famous film actress. She confided to a director that one evening Hitler had fallen to his knees and begged her to beat him. 'Lies, all lies! She begged me to beat her. When I said, "Nein," she jumped out of zer window, and vent splat on zer pavement.' This was 1937.

Her death was ruled a suicide. 'See? I vas innocent.'

There was also Gell Raisbal. Hitler established her in a Munich apartment. Hitler shot her mother-in-law. Gell and he had separate bedrooms; the carpet between was worn to shreds. She was depressed because of his insane jealousy. 'See? Mein jealousy was insane, but I was never affected.' 18 September 1931, she apparently shot herself in the chest, and apparently died. Fritz Gerlich, a journalist, claimed she was murdered. Before he could print it, Hitler shot him. At the same time, he was having an affair with a schoolteacher's daughter, Eva Braun. He showed her little affection, and flirted with other women, who found him charming despite his flabby physique, spindly limbs and rotting teeth. 'None of these descriptions are true!' He liked petite women, and blondes. 'Ya! Zat is so, like zer super race – blonde, blue eyes and big boobs, and ein gute shag! Vimin! Zey are mad for me. Hi only haff to show a little of my willy and zey are in meiner power. Three times a night is all zey need, nein?'

1932. Eva Braun attempted suicide. 'Got in Himmel, can't vimmin tink of anything else? I better treat her better. I make zer phone call. Hello, Eva, Adolf Hitler here, I hear you haff tried to commit suicide! Silly girl, look I'm going to treat you better. I am sending you ein signed photograph of me and ein bar of fruit and nut chocolate!'

On 27 February, he found a box of matches and set fire to the Reichstag, and hid. The Nazis put the blame on Red Indians. They were never caught.

In 1933 after three weeks of riots killing Chews, he took up the position of Chancellor. Von Papen, Vice Chancellor, boasted, 'Hitler was not to be taken seriously.' 'I'll haf his balls for zat.' The Riechstag fire caused Hitler to declare a state of emergency. 'Anyvun caught with ein box of matches vill haff zere balls set on fire.'

The British Army believed the Nazis had peaked, and were no longer a threat. 'That's all balls,' said Churchill.

One thing stood between Hitler and total power. Red Indians! He bypassed them, and became supreme commander and banned all other political parties, the Salvation Army, the RSPCA and the British Boxing Board.

In 1938 there were seven million Hitler Jungen. Four million who had avoided joining were forced to join, otherwise their sweet ration would be stopped, by force! He ordered the burning of books he found corrupting! All Noddy books, Bill and Ben, Winnie the Pooh, Peter Rabbit, Postman Pat, William books, Biggles. 'Avay wid zis corruption,' he said, pouring petrol on the flames and singeing his eyebrows. Faced with a severe economic crisis, he said, 'Fuck zis! I refuse to pay any Bills or Freds or Dicks or any udder names!'

The Chews

'Ya, zer Chews! I vill solve zer problem. Ve vill deport zem to Madagascar or something like that.' There was nothing like zat. 'Ach, I haff it! Ve vill put zem in camps and call them Butlins!' There were many camps called Butlins, and really bad camps were called Pontins.

'Vot is zer name on zat map, Bormann?' 'It says Poland, mein Führer.'

'Ah! Zat is a good name to declare war on!'

Suddenly he began to suffer physical illness. Being a vegetarian, he suffered bowel problems, mainly flatulence. His continual thunderous farting could clear a room in five minutes. To hold a meeting with the military, all the generals had to use clothes pegs or respirators. Plans were made to attack

Poland. Neville Chamberlain, who did Prime Minister impressions, flew to Berlin to achieve peace. 'Mein Führer, zis is Mr Chamberlain. He is zer Prime Minister of England.'

Hitler looked at a skinny man with thin neck, moustache and umbrellas.

'Are you sure, Bormann?'

'Quite sure, Führer.'

'Is he expecting rain?'

'Ze umbrella is a symbol of peace, mein Führer.'

Chamberlain held out a piece of paper. On it was written, 'Peace in our time.' Hitler read it.

'Ah, piss in our time!'

'Will you sign it, Mr Hitler?' said Chamberlain.

'I don't see vy not,' said Hitler, and put his name, Adolf Hitler. Chamberlain took the next plane home.

'Well,' said Hitler, 'zat got rid of him. Now what is zer time?' He looked at his wrist. 'Some schwein has stolen my vatch. It must be ein Chew! Kill five hundred of them. Ve haf no time to vaste, attack Poland now!'

Chamberlain stepped from his plane, waving a piece of paper, and said, 'Piss in our time,' as panzers were roaring across the

Polish border en masse. Stukas dive-bombed, Pole after Pole, till they were all gone.

The 2 Panzer under Kluge summoned the Polish Army in Dozhan and told them to surrender; they refused and told him to surrender; he refused. So these two great armies stood facing each other, refusing to surrender to each other. 14 Army under General List surrounded the Polish Army in Cracow, both refusing to surrender to each other. So the Stukas dive-bombed soldier after Polish soldier, till they were all gone.

Hitler stood in his car and blew a whistle.

'Stop zer fighting, ve haff won. Send all Chews to Butlins and Pontins . . .'

'Mein Führer, zey are all full up,' said Von Klug.

'Full up? Zen don't give them any more food.'

Chamberlain spoke on the wireless: 'As from eleven o'clock today, piss in our time has not happened so we are at war with Germany.'

'Zo, ze British vant var – zen zey will get var.'

So the British got war, six bloody years of it.

Mussolini

Mussolini was a dictator, but an idiot. 'We willa becoma a secondo Roman Umpire. I've gotta maka da war on da Wogs in Abyssinia. Using mustard gas, we beata da Wogs.

'Now we attacka da Britisha in Libya.' He did. They beat the shit out of him. He called for help. They gotta Rommel; he beat the shit out of the British. Then came Montgomery; he beat the shit out of Rommel.

Meantime, Hitler got up one morning. 'Ach, I keep forgetting to attack zer Russkies.' One thunderous fart cleared his command post. 'For God's sake, someone open ein window,' he gasped. 'Dr Morell, yew must give me anti-fart pills. Or we'll never attack zer Ruskies.'

Dr Morell did his best: he put a cork in Hitler's arse. 'That should hold for a while, mein Führer,' said Morell.

During this holding period, Hitler told his generals, 'You must attack Russia, before this cork comes out. Hardly had they attacked Russia when the cork shot out and killed Hitler's cat.

In Russia, under Guderian, the German Army advanced deep into Russia. They took

350,000 prisoners. 'Send zem to Butlins,' said the Führer.

'Zey vill haff to stand on ze udder prisoners' heads,' warned Himmler.

'Ya, zat vill make zem look taller, ha-ha,' said the Führer.

Come the Russian winter, it froze the balls off the German Army.

'Fuck zis,' said Hitler, knitting a woolly jumper for General Rommel. 'Vy are zer balls of zer Russians not frozen, Bormann?'

'Mein Führer, zey haff woollen jock straps issued by Stalin personally.'

Come summer the German colossus rolled forward. 'Mein Führer! Von Rinstead has over-run the Crimea!'

'Quick Bormann, giff him ein Iron Cross wiz oak leaves and a box of Black Magic.'

At that moment Marshall Zhukov launched a huge counter-attack. 'Hi insist no vun must retreat ein inch.' But the Russians made them retreat, one million ten thousand inches. 'Fuck zis! I must dismiss some of meiner generals. Achtung, Generals Guderian and Von Brauchitsch! You har sacked! From now hon I vill be zer Commander in Cheef ... Got in Himmel! Zoes hidiot Japanese haff bombed Pearl Harbour – for zis zer Americans vill the shit out of them beat!'

Mussolini Continued

'Madonna Mia. Those Allies have landed in Sicily, fuck it. Da king wantsa me to resign! I ama under da arresta. They are putting mea ina prigione! Aiolito!'

Hitler raged, 'Hi nefer trusted that spaghetti prick. He is full of shit and pasta. He's been haffing it orf vis Claretta Pitachi.'

Stalingrad. That name stuck in the Führer's throat. 'Zey must stand and fight to zer last man!' he raged. By now, his farting was continuous; so powerfully were they ejected that sometimes he was shot forward like a jet plane on to the wall.

'Goering, zer Luftwaffe must supply zem from zer air. Verstehen?'

Goering put the phone down, adjusted his purple silk toga, sprayed himself with exotic perfume, gave himself a shot of heroin, readjusted his gold laurel crown, threw a Rubens on the fire and warmed his jewelled hands.

'I tink he is ein goof,' said Hitler. 'Stalingrad surrendered? Nefer, Germans nefer surrender.' A fart threw him against the wall. Morell had the solution: the Führer must wear rubber bloomers with elastic waist and legs. This would seal the fart in. It did, but with each successive fart the bloomers inflated and burst. 'Fuck dis.'

He moved from his headquarters Wolfschanze (Fort Wolf) to his sumptuous retreat at Obersalzburg. He took the lift to his favourite room. He pressed a button; a screen started to ascend showing a giant glass wall revealing a sensational view.

'How about zat, Eva?'

'It is beautiful, Adolf,' she said, stripping all her clothes off and lying on the floor.

'Stop zat, Eva, you will catch your death of cold.'

His Hungarian maid Zoe set the table for tea with his favourite cream and chocolate cakes.

'Mein Führer. She wants something,' said Zoe, seeing Eva naked on the floor.

'Ya, clothes,' said Hitler. 'Perhaps,' he said musingly, 'perhaps today zat schwein Churchill will die.'

England

At that moment Churchill was in the lounge at Chartwell, sitting round a log fire, sipping champagne, at the same time finishing an oil painting. He picked up the red scramble phone.

'Hello, Harris here.'

'Ah, Harris, be a good boy and go and bomb the shit out of Berlin tonight.'

'Will do,' said Harris.

'Are you hanging up?' said Churchill.

'No, I'm standing by a desk.'

END OF PART ONE

GORILLA

I want to catch a Gorilla
As a Christmas stocking filler
I'll find one in Af-ri-ca
I'll travel there by mo-te-car
I'll look around
Till one is found
First you drug him with a dart
That will stop him for a start
Now he is unconscious on the
    ground
Oh Christ, he's coming round
Help! He's pulled off my driver's
    head

Now, now I'm sure he's dead
I no longer want a Gorilla
As a Christmas stocking filler
What I want is an empty box
    instead
So I can bury my driver's head

JOAN OF ARC

Joan of Arc
Got up in the dark
And put her foot in the Po
Oh bugger she said
Connecting with the bed
Dislocating her big toe
How can I lead France
When I lead such a dance?
Her tears were beginning to flow
To hell with le Brits
They're all a lot of shits
So now we'll give 'em a go
So she led the French Army

Half of whom were barmy
Then a terrible blow
How was she to know
The Brits beat the frogs
Who got stuck in the bogs
Joan's end was dire
The Brits set her on fire

THE QUEEN

Some people like the Queen
Or even where she's been
Some people stand and stare
In case she comes there
They don't mind seeing her from
    afar
In a distant motor car
People don't mind just missing
    her
She might be talking to Henry
    Kissinger
They bear her no malice

For living in Buckingham Palace
Some people like the Queen
Especially if she's seen

THE SUNDAY AT HOME:

A Family Magazine for Sabbath Reading.

TIGGER

Tigger my ginger cat
Somehow got bitten by a rat
So hurt was her pussy pride
She even contemplated suicide
Her pride returned
When in the house
She finally caught a mouse
When she thought that was that
She was bitten by another rat

JAM

I'm warning you Uncle Sam
Beware beware of Jam
It's always there at breakfast and
    tea
That's how it gets in you see
There is no escape from Jam
It will find you wherever you am
There's that moment of dread
When you find Jam on your bread
No matter where you are
Jam will not be very far
Dam, dam, dam, dam
Jam.

HARRODS SALE

Oh wonderful Harrods, gracing
   the street
Pushing shoving steaming feet
Sales-mad loonies care not a jot
Spending everything they've got
Look a hammock that looks nice
I've no garden but it's half-price
Buy! Buy! Corsets, carpets, a hat
And bye-bye money
That's the end of that
Carry on suckers spend the lot
Help Al Fayed buy his yacht

I CAN READ HER LIKE A BOOK $\frac{6}{10}$

S.Milligan

NOSE

This man had a big nose
It was as big as a rose
The red spread to his toes
Toes don't smell like a rose
More like cods' roes
Oh I wouldn't like those
I'd like a duck, a cat and crows
Any of those
But toes?

THEY TOLD ME YOU WERE DEAF.

Pardon?

THE HUN

I remember Hitler's stiff-armed
    salute
I remember my big army boot
My Sgt Major shout & swear
The regiment barber chopping off
    my hair
The exhausting five-mile run
All because of that bloody Hun
The early-morning bugle calls
The army had us by the balls
We were innoculated against all
    disease

Then by Christ they shipped us
　　overseas
I remember the thrill
Of life-boat drill
When they dumped us in Algiers
We all gave three cheers
We were greeted on the docks
By Arabs throwing rocks
Next we went to the front line
Many of us blown up by mine
War was no fun
All because of that bloody Hun

British Rail regret that owing to a pay dispute the next train has been sold.

S. Milligan

DONKEY

Hee Haw said the Donkey
Hee Who? said the Mule
Hee *me*, said the Donkey
That's who, you fool!

PADDY

My name is Paddy O'Hare
And sometimes I'm not there
Sometime when I feel right
I'll be on the Isle of Wight
If I'm not there I'll be
On the Isle of Innisfree
If I'm not there
I'll be elsewhere
I might also be
In the lovely vale of Tralee
I spend some time in Spain
And then move on again

I keep on moving you see
The police are after me

THE WHALE

I'd like to buy a Whale
But where are they on sale?
From what I understand
They're rarely seen on land
A Whale must be in a place
With lots and lots of space
I know where he'll be
The sea! That's it, the sea
If he's to be seen
I'll have to buy a submarine
A submarine would cost a lot
I'd have to sell everything I've got

No! No! I won't do that
Instead I'll buy a Pussy-cat

CLEVER ME

I can tell an Elephant from a Flea
How jolly clever of me
I can tell a mountain from a tram
That's how clever I am
I can tell a pimple from a spot
That's how clever I've got
I can't tell the difference from a
    Duck
Oh what bad luck

THE DUKE

The Duke of York
Refused to talk
To any of his Army

Said Sgt Glen
To some of his men
He must be bloody barmy

The Duke 'tis said
Fell on his head
While hunting in Killarney

As he died in bed
He stood on his head
And said 'Long live the stone of
    Blarney'

HIAWATHA

Hi! Hiawatha, your brother and
   your diawughter
Hi! Your tribe are living near the
   Waatha
When you marry Minne Haha or
   Mini Tee-hee
What a Ha-ha-tee-hee wedding
   that will be

Adolf Hitler
Dictator And Clown

PART TWO

Germany

'Now, Rommel, vot about zis D-day?'

'It vill come, mein Führer.'

'Yes, but ven?'

'I can't say, but ve are ready for zem. I vill be zer first to tell you, mein Führer.'

'D anke, I vill keep your secret. Tell me, how are things in Russia?'

'Very, very bad.'

'Are zey still beating zer shit out of us?'

'Ya.'

'Zere can't be much shit left.'

'No, and zer Russians haf retaken Smolensk, mein Führer.'

'Did no vun try to stop zem?'

'Ve all did.'

'Who is all?'

'Zer 2nd Panzer, 4th Panzer, XI Army, 14 Panzer, Waffen SS, X Panzer, 13 Parachute

59

Brigade, XII Panzer, XIII Panzer, Gross
Grenadier, XX Army Corps.'

'Zo zere were quite a few of you.'

Before Rommel could escape, Hitler farted.
Rommel rushed for the door. Alas, too late. It
reached him.

Moscow

Stalin sat at his desk pouring over a map. It
was soaked with vodka.

'Whatski is Generalski Timoshka doingski?'

'He is attackingski the Northern Germanski
defenceski, comrade Stalin.'

'Tell meski, is he still beating the shitski out
of themski?' 'Yeski, comrade Stalin.'

Japan

Admiral Yamamoto said, 'Amelican velly
stlong, Empelor.'

'Oh dlear, wha' can do?'

'Blugger all, my Empelor. They velly velly
stlong.'

'Blugger all, you say, Admiral?'

'Ahso, Empelor. We been knocked off
Okinawa.'

'Knocked off Fuckinawa?'
'Ahso.'

North Africa

Eisenhower sent a telegram.

```
'Montgomery you Limey bastard.
You're coming to England to lead us
on D-day.'
```

Montgomery sipped his tea, closed his bible. 'Jolly good, get Harrods to send him some chewing gum.'

General Alexander put on all his military regalia: his honours, his medals, his bottle of Scotch.

```
Your majesty, victory is mine. We are
masters of the North African shores. I
await your further orders.
   Signed Alexander the Great
```

Italy

'Helpa, helpa me, Führer,' came the wailing voice of Mussolini and spaghetti from his prison in the Grande Sanne Hotel.

A Storch plane landed outside; out stepped Otto Skorzeny. He shouted, 'Mussolini, ve haff come for you.'

Out stumbled Mussolini in an overcoat, trilby hat and some spaghetti.

'Hurry, Musso,' said Skorzeny, kicking the Duce up the arse.

Strapped in next to the pilot, who started his take-off in an alarmingly steep descent, 'Mama Mia,' shouted the Duce. 'You getta usa all fuckinga killed. I wanta getta outa.' A blow to the head silenced him and his spaghetti.

Hitler was at his house at Rastenberg; a great map was on the table. Standing round were the German high command. Unbeknown to any of zem, Count Von Staffenberg had placed a suitcase bomb under the table, then run like fuck. There was a tremendous explosion. Somewhere from the ruins, a voice said, 'Fuck zis.' It was Hitler. Seven generals were killed. Hitler was untouched. The only damage: his trousers were ripped to shreds exposing all his private parts. His hung down to his knees. Poor Eva Braun! How she must have suffered!

Mussolini arrived with his spaghetti, shaken by his terrifying journey with madmen. 'Meina Führer, whata havea you donea to youra panterloons?'

'I did nuddink, someone else did it, I'll get zer schweins.'

Mussolini saw Hitler's huge tool. 'Congratulations, meina Führer.'

Morell rushed up, saw the shattered building, saw Hitler's shattered trousers. 'Tell me, mein Führer, a fart did zis?'

'No, ein bomb.'

'So zey missed you again, nein?'

'Help! Help!' A lone German soldier in his pyjamas stood outside his bunker. 'Zer invasion has started.' He had spotted the approach of 'tousands hof ships'. Word got through to Rommel. He was asleep in bed, hugging a teddy bear. 'Hello, now hear zis. Soon zer invasion will start, try to stop them. Start by killing one called Churchill.'

The Allies stormed ashore. Tanks, taxis, Vera Lynn, Max Miller stormed inland.

Typhoons dived and machine-gunned every Kraut. 'Fuck zis,' said General Runstead.

'Mein Führer,' said Himmler. 'Vot is it now?'

'Zere are some Chews left in Warsaw!'

'Still?'

'Still.'

'Send SS Brigadier General Stroop to vipe zem out, zen send vot's left to Butlins.'

When Stroop and his SS marched into Warsaw the Chews blew them apart. 'Fuck zis,' said Stroop. 'Set fire to zer houses and hide all zer vater.'

That night Warsaw was a ruin. Only the Chewish shops were open.

Japan

'No to wolly, mline Empelor,' said Tojo. 'So we soon win war, Amelicans sullender!'

'Tojo, I hear Amelicans sink flour our airclaft calliers.'

'Ah, Empelor! We shoot tlee Amelican airclaft.'

'Shit, Tojo, you call so victory? Shit, man.'

Marine de Magio: 'Aw, they just keep coming, I shot two hundred already. I want another ice cream before they come again.'

'Banzai!!' came the roar from 50,000 Japs. The Marines blasted them for two hours.

'Man, only three of them left.'

'See? They won't quit.'

'Don't worry, de Magio, the sixteen-inch guns of the *Missouri* will stop 'em.'

The whine of a sixteen-inch shell screeched overhead, a collosal cloud of smoke obliterated the three Japs. When it cleared, one Jap was left. He shouted a hurried, 'Bugger Banzai,' and ran for it.

'I will return,' said McArthur, closing the toilet door.

Russia

Stalin's face was immobile. 'Whereski are Generals Petrov, Lanakov and General Romanov?'

'They wentski on the purge, comrade Stalin.'

'Are they all outski of Stalingrad?'

'Yes, butski they left the keys.'

'Any newski of the Czar?'

'He is still deadski, comrade Stalin.'

Germany

'Vy, vy vy? Can meiner harmy make any progress? Zey har too soft, zey need stiffening.'

'Mein Führer, zey are all frozen stiff,' said Von Below, ''ve must wait until ze summer.'

'Mein Gott, by zen zer Russian vill be in Berlin.'

Come zer spring, the Germans took Rostov, the Caucasus and the oil wells, suffering half a million casualties.

'Ve can still fill zer ranks, call up all men between eighty and ninety!'

So came into being an army of half a million, but because of heart attacks it soon came down to quarter of a million. 'I know zey don't look much, but by golly zey can fight!'

Off marched the Volksgrenadiers. The order came: 'Action stations. The Russians are going to attack.'

Three hundred Volksgrenadiers put their glasses on. The Russian army attacked. The Volksgrenadiers stood their ground. They were too old to retire. The Russians let them go with a pension.

On 25 August the Allies crossed the border into Germany. 'Fuck zis,' said Hitler. 'I vill have to leave zer Berghoff. My place is in Berlin, in zer bunker. I will win zer war from zere.'

'Of course you will,' said Bormann.

'Shut up, you prick!' screamed the Führer.

England

Churchill steadied himself and took a mouthful of caviar.

'It's not very easy to get, Winston,' said Clementine.

'How do you get it?'

'Commandos raid the coast of France.'

Churchill sipped a glass of wine. 'You know, Clemmie, France need not have surrendered. It was that awful frog woman Helene de Portes. When Reynaud was screwing her, she'd tell him to surrender to Hitler, or she wouldn't let him fuck her any more. You'd never do that to me, would you, Clemmie?' Clemmie just smiled.

July 5th, Germans launched Citadel, a pincer movement with twenty panzer divisions, Waffen SS, SS Death's Head. Little mercy was shown by either side. An extraordinary tank battle erupted, with terrible losses. The Russians took 90,000 prisoners. They hand-searched every one. They discovered 126 sauerkraut sausages and three Eva Brauns.

In the Pacific

The Americans were killing a million Japs a day.

'Hell, man,' said Admiral Nimitz. 'They must run out of them soon.' He emptied a bottle of Jack Daniel's and collapsed on the floor.

'War is hell,' said Admiral Halsey, throwing a bucket of water over the fallen figure.

'Don't,' gasped Nimitz. 'I can't swim!'

Something exploded on Halsey's head. 'Goddamn Kamikazes!' he said, brushing it away. From the command deck they could see Japan on fire and hear the screams of women and children.

'Yer know, I feel kinda sorry for them,' said Nimitz.

England

'Winston, Bomber Harris speaking. We have obliterated Dresden. There's only one post standing. Tonight we're sending a thousand bombers to destroy that.' Winston put the phone down and flicked ash off his cigar into General Alanbrooke DSO's tea.

'You swine, Churchill,' said General Alanbrooke MC DSO GIGS, and squashed a custard pie into Churchill's face, ramming his cigar down his throat.

The war was four years old.

'Happy birthday to you,' sang Montgomery MC DSO.

Hitler had been planning it for months. He had created a giant reserve Army: over a million men, ten panzer divisions, four hundred Luftwaffe planes, all to attack the Americans, defending a thinly held line pivoting on Bastagne. Montgomery had warned Eisenhower that this part of the line was very weak. 'I'm warning you, Ike, this part of the line is very weak,' he said.

'Don't take any notice of the Limey bastard,' said Patton.

'I'm not,' said Eisenhower, squeezing his lady chauffeur's tits.

The Führer stood on a mound, a stopwatch in one hand, his pocket full of sausages, and he blew a whistle. It was for the start of the Battle of the Bulge. It was 5 a.m. on December 16th. Hitler had stayed awake all night to start it. The giant army moved forward under a thunderous barrage of gunfire.

An American mayor jumped to his feet, leaving the girl on the bed. 'What the fuck was that?' He stepped outside into the snow, where he was shot dead by a German. 'That's what the fuck was that.'

To help the Americans in a desperate situation they called in the Limey General Montgomery MC DSO KG.

'Don't listen to that Limey bastard,' said Patton.

'Führer, Führer,' said Bormann. 'Deitrich has murdered some American prisoners.'

'It's zer only way to get rid of zem.'

'Vorse, mein Führer – ven General Monsteuffel told the American captain to surrender Bastogne he said, "Nuts."'

'He vill pay for zat,' said the Führer.

'Nein, he didn't pay for it, he said it for free.'

'Shit,' said the Führer.

So Bormann went for a shit. One does not disobey zer Führer.

'How is zer Pattel of zer Bulge going, Bormann?'

'Very good, mein Führer. Monsteuffel has advanced one hundred miles. He has reached Vieslam on his own!'

'Führer, ve continue pombing England,' said Goering. 'Ve will go on and on.'

'How many bombers have you?'

'Ve only haf seven left, so zey haff to keep going, coming back zen going back again.'

'But you keep missing Churchill, damn it!'

'Ya, but ve haff killed his cat.'

'Cat? Are you sure?'

'Yes, ve parachuted ein SS man carrying a tin of cat food. He put it outside zer back door of 10 Downing Street. Zer cat came; zer SS man shot it; zen someone shot him.'

'Who?'

'It was Churchill.'

END OF PART TWO

JANE

I have a divine daughter
She only drank water
Then some bloody swine
Got her into wine
Alright in its way
She drank ten bottles a day
That wasn't a sin
But my God she got into gin
Whisky by the litre
No grog could defeat her
She just couldn't resist
Getting thoroughly pissed
Then one morning at one

She became a nun
Now my divine daughter
Only drinks water

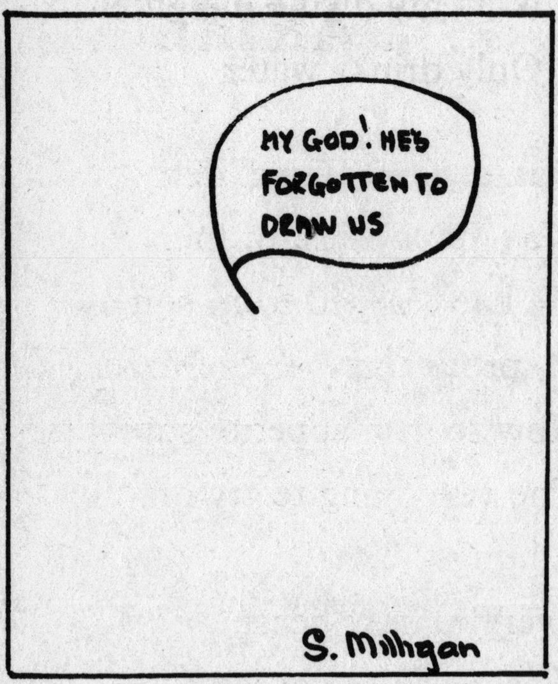
MY GOD! HE'S FORGOTTEN TO DRAW US
S. Milligan

DANIEL

Daniel in the lions' den
Was the luckiest of men
He had learned from some
   professors
How to give appetite supressors
The very thing to try on
A hungry lion
Every hungry beast
Was given one at least
By acting this way
Daniel was alive the next day

FOR SALE
BRIGHT &
Rd. £2000

FOR SALE
P.L.C.
DEAL

BEWARE
OF
VENDOR

S. Milligan.

BANANA

What a fool is the banana
Lots grow in Ghana
The banana lives in
A thick yellow skin
They can't get out
Even if they shout
The only way to reveal you
Someone has to peel you
When you are revealed
Your fate is sealed
Some hungry soul
Will swallow you whole

JESUS

Little Jesus meek and mild
Were you then an only child?
No no there was another
There was James your brother
Now when you had gone
How did James get on?
He became a solicitor
His name written on the door
And sometimes written on the
    floor
When Jesus told Pilate he was the
    son of God
Pilate said You lucky sod

Pilate knew not what to do
Said I wash my hands of you
James thought most unfair
To see his brother nailed up there
He said Jesus for a small fee
I'll have you down in time for tea
Alas poor James lost the case
Jesus was left to save the human
    race

EXPEL ELEPHANTS

Elephant Elephant

Go away

I don't like Elephants that stay

Twenty-four hours is all I can
stand

After that they must be banned

It is very well known

That England is an Elephant-free
zone

Pussy-cats and Dogs can stay

But Elephants must go away

A 'get knotted' Joke.

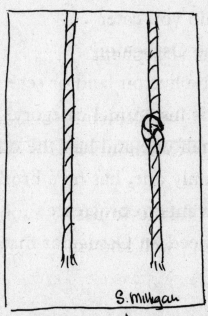

I THINK I'M
PREGNANT.

OSTRIGATOR

How do you cater
For the Ostrigator?
Does he live on land or sea?
What is his animal category?
He's half one and half the other
Is he only one, has he a brother?
If he wants to procreate
He'll need an Ostrigator mate!

CORONATION

Said Prince Charles
When they placed
The Crown on his head
I suppose this means
That Mummy's dead

FROG

Froggy Froggy
Croakity croak
Is that how
You speak or spoke?
Why are you so very fond
Of living in a smelly pond
I saw you eat a Dragonfly
If I did that
I'm sure I'd die

THE MOUSE

There was a teeny weeny Mouse
Lived in a teeny weeny house
He made a teeny weeny hole
In the cellar near the teeny weeny
    coal
At night he'd come out to have a
    teeny weeny play
He'd play a teeny weeny sax
Then someone hit him with an
    axe
It really was an overkill
But for that he'd be with us teeny
    weeny still

THE BAY

I said to the Bay of Tunisia
Have you by chance any Fish in
    here?
No there's not said the Bay
All the Fish have gone away
I have only got chips
On my dish here.

SEA

I was walking by the sea
When it splashed me
People with wet trousers
Are not welcome in people's
   houses
They might laugh at me
But I'll blame it on the sea
See?

LION

Said a man from Syon
Can you measure me for a Lion?
My inside leg is thirty-two
Said the salesman, that will never
    do
We haven't got that size Lion
Would you like an Elephant to try
    on?
No, an Elephant's too big for me
My waist is only thirty-three
Perhaps you'd like to try on a
    Gnu?

Yes, I think that will do!
Yes, he fits me perfectly
I'll take him to a Zebra tea

QUASIMODO

Quasimodo I can tell
That name rings a bell
He rings it in the Notre Dame
He rings it wherever he am
Esmerelda was the love of Quasi
But he was not good-looking was
he?

It's a blessing in
disguise

PRIZE

Solzhenitsyn got the Nobel Prize
I think that's bloody mean
Why pick bloody foreigners?
Why not Graham Greene?

LESIC LOKIT LEE

The Lesic Lokit Lee
Will be the death of me
The Lesic Lokit Lee
Is very hard to see
It attacks your head
When you're lying in bed
I foiled the Lesic Lokit Lee
By staying awake you see!

COPULATION

Means overpopulation
If you elect me
I'd introduce – vasectomy

to Canada in style,

BABU

Babu babu
Indian banker
Customers say he's just a wanker
He says, No no no I'm not
Just look at the money I've got
So the people saw the money he'd
  got
And, certainly, it was a lot

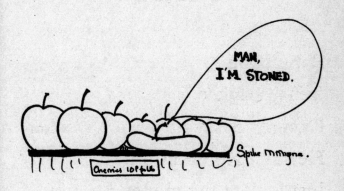

Adolf Hitler
Dictator And Clown

PART THREE

Japan

'Ah so! Amelican velly bombe Nippon, give evlebody shitees. McArthur velly stlong. He say I will return.'

'But, ha-ha, Nippon Army flighten Amelican soldiers.'

'No be flighten. Tojo velly clever.'

'Many Nippon say Tojo a clunt.'

'Ah so.'

Germany

Rommel as he had promised was on his way to tell Hitler the Allies had landed. Alas Hitler was asleep. No one dared disturb him. By the time he awoke, the Allies were ten miles in.

'Vot are you doing about it, Rommel?'

'Vell, mein Führer, I told zem to get out! You think zey would listen?'

'Haff you tried attacking zem?'

'Ya, ve did. Guess vot, zey fought back.'

Hitler gave Rommel life membership of the Masons and Manchester United. General Von Manstein took Hitler to one side.

'Mein Führer, ve are loosing tirty-tree tousand soldiers a day.'

'Zen you must look for zem!'

Italy

Mussolini and the spaghetti had been set up as head of a puppet regime in Nothern Italy. Clara Pettaci was with him. They were closely guarded by German soldiers with German servants.

'Excuse me, German servants, can you make us some spaghetti?'

'Get it yourself, einer Italian creep.'

'Mussolini, darlinga, why you letta him speak to you lika that?'

'You know, Claretta, I donta knowa. Would you like a fucka?'

'No, darlinga.'

'Do you mind if I have one?'

A German soldier warned him, 'Nix fuck vile I am on duty.'

Germany

General Branderberger rushed in, covered in mud and cowshit. 'Mein Führer, Montgomery has crossed zer Rhine.'

'Vy not? He's crossed everybody else,' said the Führer, sticking pins into the arse of a model of Churchill.

England

'Look,' said General Alanbrooke, Chief of the Imperial General Staff, 'Alex, you've got to stop going round saying you won the battle of El Alamein. You know very well General Montgomery MC DSO did it.'

'Oh, Brookie, don't be a spoilsport.'

USA

'Mister President, Mister President, we have exploded the atom bomb,' said the excited Italian scientist Nenni.

'Well, that sounds great,' said the wheelchair-bound Roosevelt. 'We better drop it on somebody.'

'How about Japan?' said the excited Italian scientist Nenni.

'Wow,' said Roosevelt, 'that's a great idea!'

Russia

'Comrade Stalinski,' said General Zhukov, 'weski are onlyski four hundred mileski from Berlinski.'

'Goodski. Giveski the troops a day offski.'

Japan

A second atom bomb was dropped, on Nagasaki. The Mayor of Nagasaki jumped to his feet. 'Wha the fluck was that?' he said.

'I tell you,' said the Mayor of Hiroshima.

Germany

Hitler sat on the Chancery toilet, straining, straining, straining. His eyes stood out like organ stops.

'Hurry up in zere,' said Herman Goering. 'I've got dysentery.'

'You lucky bastard,' said Hitler.

★ ★ ★

Eva Braun stood naked looking at her reflection in the mirror. 'Vy vy doesn't he fuck me?'

'He's only got a small willy,' said Dr Morell. 'Maybe he's fucked you and you haven't noticed it.'

Japan

'My Empelor, my Empelor!' said Tojo.

'There only one of me, which Empelor you want?'

'Empelor, we must sullender before next bluddy atom bomb.'

'Ha we got tlime?'

'Yes. I glot time. It twenty past tlee.'

Ireland

Jasus,' said De Valera. 'Der Germans are bombing London to bits. Tell der IRA to stop.'

England

Churchill had just finished painting Lady Astor. 'She said if I was her husband she'd poison my coffee. I said, "If I was your husband I'd drink it!" ' He emptied a bottle of champagne over the dwarf Lord Beaverbrook.

'How nice of you to remember me, Winston,' he said.

Belgium

The British Parachute Brigade were dropped at Arnhem to take the bridge. This was the fifth day and they hadn't taken it. They were under unending attack from two hundred panzer divisions. The Brigade, despite valiant resistance, received no relief. As a special privilege, Monty dropped them the football results.

'Fuck this,' said General John Frost, DSO MC CB, swallowing a tin of bully beef. 'Blast, I forgot to open the tin.'

'You'll get the VC for that,' said Captain Logan, DSO RAMC.

Germany

Hitler was reviewing his SS Werewolf Death's Head soldiers. He stopped in front of an Oberleutnant. Not is your name?'

'Meiner name is Schitz, Herman Schitz.'

'Schitz?' said Hilter.

'Ya, Schitz. All my family are Schitz. They come from a long line of Schitz. There have been many Schitz in zer Army.'

'Gute,' said Hiter, 'the more Schitz zer better.'

'Heil Hitler,' said Schitz.

As best she could, Fräulein Manzialy arranged three peas, a date and a prune on a plate. 'Dinner, mein Führer,' she said.

Hitler took the plate. 'Oh yum, yum, ein feast. Vot is for afters?'

'Ein cherry,' she said.

'Ach, life is gute,' he said. 'I'll have a glass of water to wash it all down.'

He sat in the little café at Berchtesgarten, eating cream cakes. 'Zat is zer thirty-second cream cake, Adolf,' said Eva Braun.

'Oh, doesn't time go quickly ven you are having fun.' Suddenly he stopped. 'Eva, get out!' he said. 'Quickly, you haven't a minute to lose.' Eva rushed out. Hitler farted. The effort overwhelmed him. He collapsed on the floor. 'Help,' he said weakly. 'Open all zer windows and doors!'

Firemen wearing gas masks carried him to safety. 'He can't go to parties like zis,' said one.

While Hitler slept in the corner of an upright sofa, the Russian army advanced in millions on Germany. Even when he was awake the Russians advanced in millions on Germany. He spent his time throwing a stick for his dog Blondi to retrieve. After throwing it two hundred times, he kicked Blondi's arse. 'Vy do you keep bringing it back?' he shouted. His hair was lank, his eyes dull, spit dribbled from the corner of his mouth, his left hand had a tremor, his left leg had a tremor. He controlled it by tightly tying it to a piano leg. His diet consisted of very thin pea soup.

'Will he ever get better?' said Eva to Dr Morell.

'Not under me, he won't,' he said.

'Vot are zose injections you giff him?' she said.

'Pea soup,' he said.

The old boy General Montgomery MC DSO, Knight of the Garter, said, 'I want to take Berlin.'

'Over my dead body,' said Ike.

So Montgomery shot him and stepped over his dead body on his way to Berlin. (In fact

Montgomery never shot Eisenhower, but he would have loved to.)

'Winston,' said Bomber Harris. 'I want to be seconded to God. As soon as I am, I will send a million bomber raids on Dresden.'

'I'll talk to my war cabinet tomorrow,' said Churchill. 'I'll see what I can do. Montgomery has asked me to do exactly the same for him.'

Montgomery's 21st Army group had surrounded Hamburg. The only escape was upwards. 'General, General,' gasped General Horrocks. 'They are escaping upwards.'

'Arrest them as they come up,' said Monty.

'Mein Führer! Mein Führer!' gasped Bormann. 'Hess has flown to England on einer peace mission!'

'Oh?' said the Führer. 'Is he coming back?'
'No.'

'No? Vy dos he vant to live in Hingland? Zey are ze bloody henemy. Vere his he staying? Zer Ritz?'

'Vormwood Scrubs Prison, Mein Führer!'

Hitler took a custard pie and threw it at Bormann's face. Splat! It hit him square on.

'Zere. That's vot I tink of Hess.'

* * *

'Fire,' said Hitler standing on a stool. Flames spread from the ascending V1 rocket. 'Zat vill be a surprise for Churchill. Ha-ha,' he said, pitching head first off the stool.

England

Churchill sipped his champagne. He heard a strange drone approaching. Through a window he saw his first VI rocket. 'Good heavens. Will that Nazi swine never stop? Fuck him!'

As the Führer's head hit the ground, the VI exploded on Wells & Co. jam factory in Barnsley. It stopped production. A terrible blow to a country dependent on jam for living.

Churchill spoke on the wireless: 'My fellow countrymen, it is with heavy heart that I tell you that Wells & Co. jam factory has stopped production, but this will not stop us! We will fight them in the streets without jam! We will fight them in the hills without jam! We will fight them to the end without jam!'

Germany

The Führer lay unconscious on the ground after his fall. Regaining consciousness, he said, 'Vot vos dat?'

'That vos you, mein Führer,' said scientist Von Braun.

'Vat happened?'

'You happened, Führer.'

'You look very tall, Von Braun.'

'That's because you are lying down, Führer.'

As the first Russian shell landed on Berlin, Hitler ran into the bunker and slammed the door. 'For Gott's sake, Führer, please don't fart in here,' pleaded Dr Morell. 'Hi will have to put zer cork back in with a two-minute warning siren, zat vill giff us a chance to get out.'

Duly the Führer was fitted with the cork. 'Hit giffs two minutes' warning, you say?' he said.

'Is it comfortable?' said Dr Morell.

'No. It feels as if hi haff zomething stuck up meiner arse,' Hitler said.

The cork seemed to be working, but everyone in the bunker was on tiptoe waiting to rush out with the two-minute signal. They all wondered if there would be enough warning! Every eye was focused on Hitler's arse. Mid-morning, suddenly the siren started. In two minutes the bunker was empty. It would take half an hour to clear. Those waiting outside were being shelled by Russian guns.

'Hiff ve stay up here ve vill be killed,' said Bormann.

'If we go down zere, ve vill die,' said Speer.

They counted half an hour. 'Now it is safe.'

They entered the bunker. Hitler was unconscious, rendered so by his own fart. Delicately, Dr Morell reinserted the cork, and reset the alarm. At that moment they were joined by Eva Braun. 'Vot is wrong vid mein Adolf?'

'He just farted, Fraulein,' said Speer.

'Oh, mein poor Adolf. Farting is his curse,' she said.

'His and ours,' said Bormann.

The phone rang. It was for the Führer. 'Führer, here. Who is it?'

'It's Admiral Doenitz, Führer. I'm afraid ze Pritish and zer Americans are sinking our submarines in large numbers, last month – one hundred and twenty.'

'I haff zer answer. Stop sending zem out.' The Führer hung up. 'Now we must prepare for battle. Get out ze maps.'

Dutifully the maps were laid out. 'Fools,' he screamed. 'Zese are map routes of Lewisham district 49A buses.'

'Zese are Luftwaffe maps.'

'Oh. Zen we must giff zem orders to bomb all 49A buses in Lewisham. Ve vill bring Pritish transport to ein halt. Churchill will have to bloody well walk.' He smashed a fist into his hand. This was the first sign of Hitler's insanity. Far worse was the evening he would appear with a floral dress, fishnet stockings and high-heeled shoes. 'Now who vill dance vid me?'

Speer danced with him. 'If Churchill could see me now,' he mused.

By morning Hitler had reverted to normal. 'You were lovely last night, mein little Führer,' said Speer.

Two German pilots flew into the bunker. One was an excitable woman pilot, Hanna Rietsch, and Ritter von Greim. 'Führer, we love you,' said Rietsch, 'and will stay to the end.' Wrong! Von Greim did not want to stay to the end. No. He had only come to say goodbye and fuck off.

The Americans and Russians had met on the River Elbe and started shooting each other. 'Now, Goddamn it, that's enough,' said Patton. So they stopped. They exchanged cigarettes, chewing gum, coloured beads, hand mirrors, toilet paper, film stars, women and tanks.

The Chews were still in Butlins and Pontins camps. Next day, Goddamn it, General Patton, in a tank, let them out. 'Any Limey bastards here?'

'No, there aren't.'

'What rotten bloody luck,' he said, shooting some Chews instead.

Hitler marched up and down, pulling the piano with him. 'Vere is Wenke vid zer relief army?' Russian shells were dropping on the bunker. Any minute Russians would burst in.

'Mein Führer,' said Bormann, 'you must hide. Hide under zer gas stove.'

'Nein. I don't vant to be taken prisoner with ein gas stove,' said Hitler. 'First I must marry Eva.'

At three in the morning Adolf married Eva. They gathered their friends around them and drank still water till five in the morning. 'Aren't you going to fuck her?' said Bormann.

'I already haff, but she hasn't noticed it. Now I must blow my brains out.' Hitler tried three times to blow his brains out and missed. Dr Morell made a cross where he thought

Hitler's brain was. This time he hit it. Both he and Eva were laid in the garden, doused with petrol and set on fire. Goebbels did a prawn barbecue on them.

At Lüneberg the German generals surrendered to General Montgomery. 'Tell these chaps I want them to sign their names in English as I don't speak German. Now give each of them a hypodermic of NAAFI tea.'

Poor Rommel, he never lived to see all this. He had been driven to a forest and forced to drink a poisoned cup of Horlicks. But for the rest of her life Frau Rommel kept an oil painting of a large Horlicks tin over her bed.

Churchill spoke on the wireless: 'That Narzi chap, Hitler, is dead. I have sent his relatives condolences on a piece of toilet paper. All Narzis will be hung for twenty-four hours. God save the King and my brandy!'

THE END

TWIT

James Warrington Wit
Was an upper-class twit
Why it's hard to say
An upper-class yob
Without a job
A layabout all day
He lay about in Chatham
Lewisham as well
He lay about in Clapham
As to why it is hard to tell
James Warrington Wit
Didn't care a bit

What other people said
And went this way
All his life they say
Until the day he was dead

NEW BALLS

New balls said the Emperor
On the tennis court
New balls said the Equerry
Your Majesty what sort?
Tennis balls you fool
The only other sort
Are hanging from your tool
Men with no balls by choice
Have a very high voice

FAMILY

Oh dear Oh dear
My mum is so fat
She wears huge knickers
And that is that

Yet my dad
Is very thin
The letterbox is
How he gets in

My brother Jim
Is six foot seven
Sees Angel feet
Up in heaven

My sister Sue
Is very small
I trod on her in the hall

Oh dear Oh dear
Oh dearie me
What a strange family

I DREAMED

I dreamed that I was somewhere
    else, but where?
I looked around but nobody was
    there!
While I was somewhere else with
    little to do
So I added one plus one and it
    came to two
Next I met a little man who had
    passed on
I often wonder where is, or where
    he had gone

I awoke one morning at the break
of day
The morning was sunlit and
sublime
So then I hadn't been somewhere
else
I'd been here all the time

MORE JAM

I hate Jam
I don't want it to know where I
    am
I want a Jam-free life
Never letting Jam on my knife
Beware of Jam my friend
It can spread from end to end
Eating Jam is a sin
Letting all that Jam go in
Let your life be pure like me
Totally, totally, Jam free
Be careful my friend
Or Jam will get you in the end

GERMAN
SOLDIER

I am a German soldier
I like to go to war
And when zat war is over
I go and look for more
And ven zat war wus over
I cried and cried and cried
Some British swine had shot me

Because of zat, I died

THIS WAY TO
HERE.

S. Milligan.